Staying Motivated

A Complete Self-Control Guide on How to Boost Willpower and Develop Mental Strength

Andrew D. Hoskins

Your Gift!

We want to show our appreciation that you support our work,
so we have put together a gift for you.
Just visit the link on the last page of this book to download it
now.
We know you will love this gift.
Thanks!

Table of Content

Introduction

"We have forty million reasons for failure,
but not a single excuse."
-Rudyard Kipling

Every person has a goal in life or has something to do. It's a motive that drives you to invest, spend time, and even money into a project or business.

This person dreams of becoming rich, famous, powerful, or simply want to have a healthy life, few problems, a fixed income and avoid all the trouble. Every person wants to accomplish professionally and humanly differently; there is no rule in this.

But there is something that can make a difference, something that can turn an average person into a successful person, something that can push our friend to reach the goal, not to give up in a time of difficulty and always commit to ending what he started.

This force has a name; it allows to get great results, to move mountains.

This force has a name; it is called Motivation.

Motivation is that power that allows every person to continue to struggle and work to achieve a goal.

This goal can be a graduation, getting a job promotion, writing a book, losing weight, learning to do something, engaging, conquering the world, anything.

Motivation drives us never to give up, to react to negative criticism, to think positive, and to always give the best.

Motivation is the difference between success and failure.

People who have a high motivation or who know how to handle it have greater chances of achieving their goals than a person who can not handle criticisms and unforeseen events.

In this book we will find out how to handle motivation, to be motivated and ready to win every challenge.

Nothing and no one will be able to destroy your motivation because you will know exactly what you want and how to achieve your goals.

Finally able to stop thinking about a sentence, the worst sentence in the world, a phrase that I hate with all my strength.

The phrase is "Why am I doing it?"

This sentence is devastating because it is capable of destroying all your motivation in one second, canceling all the efforts and everything you have accomplished so far. This sentence can give birth to doubts and insecurities; it is your enemy, this sentence should never be spoken or thought, is a poison and motivation is our antidote.

Thanks to the right motivation you will be able to answer this question and destroy all your doubts.

You will go to the mirror and speak with your mind.

"Why are you doing it?"

"Because my goal is to lose weight."

"All you do is useless; you will never lose weight, the girls laugh at you" here are the insecurities.

"It is not true; my goal is to lose weight for my health. The opinion of others does not mean anything to me."

"All you do is useless. Within a month you will come back to eating burgers and cakes" here are the doubts.

"It is not true because I have a great ally, the MOTIVATION."

"The motivation?"

"Yes, thanks to the motivation, I will not abandon the diet after a month, and I will lose weight. No doubt or insecurity will stop me."

This dialogue can adapt to all your goals and serves to show that often the true enemy is inside ourselves.

There is a force in our head, the one that leads us to procrastinate, who is afraid of changes, be motivated means to change our habits, to be able to adapt to changes and improvise solutions, to exit the comfort zone that we have built over the years.

This voice in our heads is afraid of change, even though it may produce positive effects and stops us.

The change always scares, and people who can not handle the motivation will be frightened, missing the opportunity to improve their lives.

But reading this book you will discover how to turn off this item and just listen to the motivation, and the next chapter will learn a great motivational story.

Chapter 1 – Arthur Boorman

"Life is 10% what happens to you and 90% how you react."
           -Anonymous

The name of Arthur Boorman is perhaps not very familiar, but it is the perfect motivation story to start this book.

Arthur is a former soldier, a disabled veteran of the first Persian Gulf War. The damage was done in the war, together with several injuries prevented him from returning to live a normal life, and soon Arthur has lost all sorts of motivation. The lowest point was touched on February 9, 2007, when Arthur weighed nearly 300 pounds. Arthur could barely walk using crutches and a bust for the back. Even dressing had become hard, and Arthur felt humiliated to ask for help to carry out the simplest tasks.

At that moment Arthur understood that he had to change his life, but no personal trainer wanted to deal with him. Arthur was a lost war, and nobody wanted to waste time with him. But Arthur had found the motivation, and his goal was to change his life forever, abandoning crutches.

Arthur was able to contact Diamond Dallas Page, a retired wrestler, and inventor of DDP Yoga, a new fitness method. Page was always a great motivational speaker, he began his training to become a professional wrestler when he was 35 years old when many athletes started to think about retirement, and he never gives up, becoming a world champion.

Back problems forced him to retire in 2002, and Page developed his training method, the DDP Yoga.

DDP was the only one who wants to deal with Arthur's problem, teaching them the basic exercises of the DDP Yoga.

Arthur started performing only the exercises he was able to do, slowly increasing the difficulty of the tasks and thanks to this commitment and a proper diet was able to reach 197 pounds. The training was difficult, but the motivation of Arthur has always been high, and at the end, when he was able to run without corsets for the back or crutches he felt like the king of the world.

Think of this story and what you can accomplish with the power of motivation, and take an example from Arthur's story to improve your life effectively.

Chapter 2 – Two types of motivation

"The biggest waste in the world is the difference between what we are and what we could become."
-Ben Herbster

Until this point, we spoke about motivation without giving a precise definition.

Motivation is not a miracle, something falling from the sky or that you can find under the bed, but it is a state of mind that you must build one brick at a time with determination, consistency, and willpower.

If you hoped to find the magic formula A + B = C to get the motivation, I give you my most sincere excuses, because unfortunately in this book you will not find any magic formula, but only the best methods to improve your motivation. These are methods that require your maximum commitment and need time and constancy to produce results.

Motivation, or other life outcomes, are not built with easy methods or shortcuts, in personal growth if someone proposes an easy method, it's a scam, knowing ourselves and improving takes time, but at the end of the path, the results are guaranteed.

Continuously improving by following a method without never giving up is a real sample of motivation.

The word motivation comes from the Latin "movere" which means moving because it is the push that makes us act. In other words, motivation is like fuel. Without gasoline, the car does not start, and without motivation, you will also be struggling to get started or to start one of your projects.

Motivation is fundamental in different areas of life.

If you are a teacher, you will know how difficult it is to motivate those students who have no intrinsic motivation.

In the field of work, for decades, leaders have assumed that the best way to motivate their employees is by promising them financial gain or threatening them with loss of work ignoring what the real motivational motives of their employees are. Often CEO and leaders confuse the threats with the motivation in the workplace, and the only result will be to make people working in a climate of fear, rather than in a creative atmosphere, burying the motivation of each employee.

Motivation, therefore, serves as "fuel" to achieve goals. These goals can be complex or simple; no goal is ridiculous or useless because every person has the right to feel accomplished the way he or she prefers.

So the motivation allows us to create a business, to have healthy social relationships, but also simply to get up in the morning to go to work even if we carry out a job "humble" (bullshit, no honest work is humble).

There are two types of motivation, the intrinsic and the extrinsic ones.

Intrinsic motivation is a motivation that starts from within us, especially when we are involved in something that can solicit our interest.

Surely you will have noticed that if something interests you, you are more motivated to do it (a person who loves the gym will attend it every day without problems) because this activity can stimulate your intrinsic motivation.

The individuals who have a high intrinsic motivation always succeed in producing better results than others in their tasks and they are becoming more and more involved because they feel that that activity is both stimulating and self-motivating. Intrinsic motivation is therefore strongly related to the type of business you carry out. If you can not find it interesting in any way, it will be difficult always to be stimulated and motivated to do well. In this case, you need to find some positive aspects in the activity and focus on those rather than thinking about the negative aspects.

What to do if you can not find something positive? Unfortunately, there are no solutions, except to abandon this activity (if possible) or job to follow something that interests us most.

Extrinsic motivation is the set of all the external factors that can motivate a person. These factors can be awards, reinforcements or gratifications.

For example, a salesperson will try to sell more and more products to get the monthly prize (a monetary bonus, for example) or a person can devote himself to fitness to have a better body and to please more people (in this case for personal gratification).

Students have a lot of extrinsic motivation, especially on subjects that don't interest or they do not feel important for their future. In this case, the extrinsic motivations are the graduations and prizes they can obtain.

It is often believed that extrinsic motivations are stronger because they are generated by external factors that affect everyone, such as money.

Money has always been considered the greatest motivation in the world. People do jobs that they hate because they need money, or do humiliating or dangerous activities to have a higher salary.

Money is a motivation you can touch; you can use all over the world and you that you can turn into something else. Saying "I do it for the money" is considered healthy while saying "I do it because I like it" is treated as an immature phrase.

This conviction, however, has been denied by some research, which has shown that emotional motivations are often stronger than material ones, such as money, and in particular, the most powerful emotions are those that make us want the approval of other people.

The example of the person practicing fitness to have a better body to please the people is perfect, but even an employee who works hard to have the boss's approval is a perfect example.

People are often moved by external factors such as awards, titles, ratings, opinions that others may have of them.

People can also be motivated by emotions that arise within them, that concern only them, as interest, curiosity, the desire to help others or deep values. These are all intrinsic motivational factors and can support passions, hobbies, and efforts.

According to Deci and Ryan's Self-determination theory, there are three natural needs whose satisfaction increases intrinsic motivation. This theory identifies three psychological needs: the need for competence, independence, and connection.

First, people want to raise their skills.

Companies often believe that the only way to meet this need of the employees is through a promotion. Deci found that giving excellent positive feedback on a task to people increased their intrinsic motivation to do the job because it pleased their need for competence.

Other researchers instead observed that the negative feedback have the opposite effect (decreasing the intrinsic motivation by turning off the need for competence).

Evidently, these people perceive this negative feedback as a failure, and this leads to a decline in self-esteem and motivation. In this case, it is critical to have the humility to hear negative feedback and to learn from your mistakes.

People are also motivated by being independent, but a salary increase does not always lead to greater independence, though it is a factor that can stimulate it. Independent means making decisions without supervision and control of others.

Finally, connection sensations. People need to experience a sense of belonging and attachment to other people to be motivated.

The theory of self-determination, in other words, makes us understand how important it is for personal growth to make autonomous choices, to feel competent in what we do and belong to a group.

A team that feels connected, with complicity and team spirit will work much better and will be more motivated to a group of people who only think about their success.

For example, think of a soccer team. If the team is motivated and playing correctly and without self-centering, the team will be able to produce more results than a team where every player thinks only about his success.

Two great emotional levers to be known to be motivated are pleasure and sorrow.

In the end, all the actions we do are driven by only two feelings, feel pleasure or avoid pain.

Think about the decisions you have taken in your life. You will find that behind most of your choices there was a more or less conscious push to move to some form of pleasure or to avoid some pain.

Although seeking for happiness is one of the strongest motivational levels, pain is more useful in creating behavioral changes. It is no coincidence that many people undertake personal change paths after a major emotional trauma, such as the end of a relay or mourning.

But pain is a short-term motivator, while we need a long-term motivational agent and can only find it by pursuing the level of pleasure that is the basis of intrinsic motivation. A longer path, but it will bring long-term results.

The problem is that most of us base their decisions on how to create pleasure (or avoid pain) in the short term rather than in the long run.

This is partly attributable to modern society, which has accustomed people to seek immediate motivations and satisfactions instead of planning a long-term outcome, it is better to have the egg today instead of the hen tomorrow.

As Tony Robbins explains, when you do something you know is wrong for you in the long run but enjoyable in the short term (e.g., drinking alcohol, smoking, ...), the best way to make changes in yourself is to create so much pain in your mind around that thing, so you have no choice but to take the decision to change.

For example, this is why government and cigarette companies print photos with cancer and mining messages on cigarette packets. They are trying to create a pain associated with the cigarette pack to provide the best motivation to quit smoking.

Chapter 3 – The 10 Steps to be always motivated – featuring willpower

"Only one thing makes a dream impossible: the fear of failure."

-Paulo Coelho

Thanks to my experience I managed to develop ten steps to be motivated or to find motivation again after a difficult time.

These ten steps are not magic, but only instructions to change your mindset and your lifestyle, as I have already written, I do not sell instant magic formulas because I do not want to cheat anyone.

These ten steps require the usual dedication, humility, sincerity, but above all a lot of willpower. Knowing how to manage motivation is a delicate task, which must be constant and that is likely to stop at any time, especially due to independent external factors beyond our control.

For this reason having a great willpower can make us a leap of quality in the development of motivation, so you need to understand how to have a strong willpower.

In a nutshell, the willpower is the ability to say "NO" to temptation, have clearly in mind a project and continue the path to achieve it despite the difficulties.

Willpower is training with discipline and with some small tricks, one of the most unusual, but which has high psychological effectiveness is to enter into a contract with ourselves.

Write a document where you are committed to making certain actions, sign it and print it out so that you can always see it. Establish penalties in case of non-fulfillment and try to comply with that contract every day.

Respect the sanctions in the event of non-fulfillment, and in a short time, you will notice that you will become more determined to respect it by increasing your willpower.

Do a work of self-analysis (sincerity, I recommend), identifying your weaknesses. You are the only one who knows them, and you are the only one who can change them, but to do that you have to have the humility and sincerity to recognize them.

After identifying the weaknesses, you can correct them by working with will power, relying on your desire for change. You can start this process by eliminating unnecessary activities that make you lose much time or harmful food activities.

Train your will every day with little challenges, for example, not eating your favorite food and replacing it with fruit, or with something you do not like very much. Obviously at the beginning will not be easy to change, but willpower will help you in this challenge allowing you to meet this commitment. In a few days, you will discover that this change will not be more painful and will be much more natural.

All these simple exercises can help you improve your willpower, but the principle of change must take place within you. Otherwise, all these activities will be useless, a waste of time.

The engine of change, willpower and motivation are within us.

If we want to improve our lives and carry out personal growth, then we will make a difference. Otherwise, all we do is useless. So you continue to read only if you want to try changing; otherwise, any path will have the only result of losing time and money. Instead, if you are motivated to change your life the best way, you continue to read, and you will find that being motivated is easy.

Now is the time to embark on the path with ten steps to stay motivated and to find motivation again.

I repeat once again; these steps are mental exercises, no miraculous intervention but only activities that you can do to increase your motivation. There are no shortcuts in this activity, and for this reason, the route must be planned to have long-term results.

So, if you want an immediate result or a magic word, I renew the invitation to stop reading now, so you do not waste time. But for those who want to improve and get a serious result, in the long run, this is the best way to be determined and never lose the motivation despite everything.

1- Start

Many times we procrastinate, and we do not even start a project, even though we have so many things in mind. Motivation is often stimulated by the pursuit of activity that we like and who can enjoy us.

For this reason, the first step to be motivated or to find the motivation is to start the activity that we want without mental problems and without ridiculous apologies to postpone it again.

Wear your sneakers and go to the gym, start studying or start working. In this way, you will turn the engine of your motivation, and after a concise time, everything will be more natural.

The most important thing in this step is to not think about what we are doing.

Do not reflect on how much you are demotivated, do not think "why do I do this?", Do not think about quitting as soon as possible, the only thing you have to think is to start in the best way. In this way, your mind will automatically eliminate the negative thoughts, the lack of motivation and the temptation to procrastinate everything.

Remember that there is a force inside you that will try to stop you, and all the negative thoughts are fuel for this enemy and will allow him to find plenty of good reasons to keep you from starting your activity.

So, stop stay on the couch and starts to do something, motivation is around the corner.

2 - Turn your goals into smaller actions

Often we have very ambitious targets (it is not wrong, ambition is a strong motivator), but these goals are too ambitious and cause us to lose any motivation quickly when we see that we have no positive results in the short term.

To try to counter this problem, the best solution is to take our goal and divide it into so many smaller actions that you can handle better. Try to devote a maximum of one hour of time to each action so that you can play differently during the day.

For example, our goal is to go to the gym and develop a beautiful body. Obviously, the results will only be visible after a long time, and so many people abandon the gym.

Take your goal and divide it into several smaller goals, such as

- ***100 push-ups per day***
- ***Running three times a week***
- ***Working out with weights twice***

This way you can choose which goal to complete each day (the goals must be simple, the goal is to simplify everything) considering the time available. Choose tasks that can lead to short-term visible results (for example, you will have a better cardio in a short period) and this will help you stay motivated.

3 - Set a deadline

Scientific research shows that people are much more motivated when they have a deadline. This expiration prompts them to work fast and not to procrastinate anything. Some people appreciate being constantly under pressure because they feel high motivation in the challenge.

The sense of urgency and the challenge are two great motivators because they stimulate our sense of competition with others and with ourselves. We must be able to win this challenge with ourselves and win every challenge. This system is also very efficient for self-esteem. Being able to meet a deadline means that we have worked well, intelligently and correctly managing the time at our disposal.

Positive feedback is the right crowning of this goal, the correct acknowledgment to our commitment. Without a deadline, our attitude will be more relaxed, and we may lose the motivation because we do not have the sense of urgency, but with a time limit, it is a race against time, an excellent training for our motivation.

4 - Do not go too fast

When we start a project, our motivation is at its best, and we are ready to break the world. This excessive motivation can be very dangerous.

It seems like a paradox, but being too motivated is very counter productive because too much motivation can lead us to want to overdo and want to do too many things at the beginning of the project. This desire to exaggerate may result in too much work and consequently to fatigue and to lose our motivation when we can not make progress or properly manage every task.

My personal story. I was motivated to enroll in the gym and to attend a dance course.

I wanted to do everything in the same month because my motivation was at its best. A friend was able to convince me not to go too fast.

"You can not handle so many things at the same time. Choose a task and start with that. Next month you will start the other"

"But I'm motivated."

"Yes, it is true, but you can not handle so many things at the same time. The only result you achieve is to waste time and not to achieve a task in the right way."

My friend was right, and I decided to go to the gym the first month, learning how to handle time. The following month I joined the dance course and already knew how to manage the time properly.

If I decided to do everything together, because of too much motivation I would have given up everything after a few months because of too many commitments together.

Then choose one project at a time, without exaggerating, you do not have to prove anything to anyone, the only goal is to carry out the task properly to be motivated.

5 - Record your progress

Observing progress is a rocket for motivation, there is no better thing to see the results of a project and to feel appreciated. Keeping a diary or a calendar where to note all progress made in the project is very effective in maintaining motivation and constantly being encouraged to continue the journey.

For example, if your goal is to lose weight, record your weight every week, and every time you notice progress your motivation will go to the maximum. Additionally, this activity will become a routine, and you will not be able to record your progress every day.

There are also sites to help you score your progress as http://www.joesgoals.com/

6 - A prize

Being rewarded (for example with feedback) is very important to be motivated. Everyone loves to be appreciated (we saw the intrinsic and extrinsic motivation) and have an award is a great incentive for motivation.

Whenever you start a project, set a prize and some intermediate prizes when you can make the challenges. Make sure to reward you every time, and you will notice that the satisfaction of getting the award will help to keep you motivated.

7 - Why

We started this book with the question "Why do you do it?" Well, when you start the project you have to write ten reasons that will push you to start and finish that task. Write why you do it, what you want to achieve and imagine what will you do once you reach the desired result.

As you write, I'm sure you will feel the motivation to grow within you.

In this case, you can exaggerate and write everything you want; the important thing is to keep the motivation to the maximum and to imagine the treasure at the end of the rainbow is a great motivation.

8 - Use the pictures

Photos can help us remember people or happenings. In this case, they can help us remember our goal. Collect photographs that can remind you of your goal (things, individuals or objects) and place them so that you can always see them (such as the phone's wallpaper or a custom desktop wallpaper for example). These photos will be a great boost to your motivation.

In this way, you will avoid that your inner enemy uses his tricks to make you forget about your goal.

9 - 5 Minutes Motivation

Often our days are very hectic, and we can not focus on our goal.

For this reason, the motivation must continuously be trained. Use your smartphone and dedicate 5 minutes a day to meditation. Listen to a song, a meditation music or a motivational monologue (Al Pacino in "Any Given Sunday" is my favorite) as you think of your goal.

5 minutes of pure motivation.

10 - Involve another person

Often we can not achieve our goals. That is why we have to include other people, friends or partners.

My personal experience: when I was racing with a friend his presence motivated me to keep running even if I was tired, so I overcame my limit.

Talk about your project to your partner or a loved one, outrun the strategy and the benefits you will get. His or her support will be a great motivation, and the fear of disappointment will help you stay motivated. Sharing ideas, dreams, and ambitions help to create a climate of complicity and motivate together.

Conclusion

"Twenty years from now you will be more annoyed by the things you did not do than by the ones you did. So spring the moorings, get out of the safe harbor and let the wind swell your sails. Explore. Dream. Discover."
-Mark Twain

The motivation is very delicate. It takes a long time to be built and can be destroyed in a second.

Being constantly motivated requires so much work and a great willpower, but following these tips, you will always be motivated and full of energies.

The goals of our lives are not accomplished on their own, commitment and dedication are needed, and thanks to this book, motivation will no longer be a problem.

Your Gift!

We want to show our appreciation that you support

our work, so we have put together a gift for you.

bit.ly/2u7pdNL

Just visit the link above to download it now.

We know you will love this gift.

Thanks!